My name is Gloria Phillips. I am a proud Gumbaynggirr Elder from Coffs Harbour, on the Mid-North Coast of New South Wales. When I was a young girl, I lived with my parents and eight siblings. I also had an older brother, Tony who had to leave home to find work in Sydney where he joined the army.

We lived at Pipeclay which is now known as Corindi. Corindi is named for the clay found in the area. It was used in traditional ceremonies for men and women.

Dad and Mum moved to Corindi because of family and cultural connections. The community was settled on Crown Land. Other families lived nearby and they were also close kin.

My father, Thomas built a house made of bark. It was right on the banks of a large lake. He was employed as a timber cutter and knew the best wood to use. It never leaked once from the rain. Our mattresses were made from chaff sacks. These were once hessian potato bags that we stuffed with dried grass. Our pillows were made from washed flour bags. We filled these with old rags to make them soft.

We had no electricity and used fat lamps at night. We also had a dirt floor. In the kitchen, we had an open fire. A tripod with a camp oven hung over the open fire for cooking.

There was a shop about 5kms away, over the sand dunes. We were able to book up food at the shop until Mum's endowment cheque arrived. We didn't have the same luxuries as those people living in town, but we had each other.

PIPECLAY
GENERAL STORE

We also had a large, extended family of cousins, aunties, uncles and grandparents. Any household items that were not needed by one family were always passed on to others. Nothing was wasted.

The whole family always shared any food that was caught. The lake provided plenty of food for us, which we cooked on the outside fire over the hot coals. We caught tailor, flathead, bream, blackfish, mullet, whiting, crabs, oysters and prawns.

Being the eldest child, one of my jobs was to look after my younger siblings. One of my strongest memories was when my three year old brother Peter, and his dog Patch, wandered off. The whole family started worrying and Colin raced to the beach to try and find him. Thankfully he did, because Peter was only little and couldn’t swim.

When Colin returned from the beach with Peter and Patch, he told us how Patch would push Peter back towards the shore each time he tried to wander too close to the waves. Thank goodness for Patch! Everyone was so relieved that Peter was safe and back home with his family. Patch was rewarded with a large kangaroo bone that night for his dinner.

I have many happy memories of growing up in Pipeclay. We spent time with our family and friends fishing, singing, story-telling, dancing, swimming, hunting and gathering. Even though times were hard, we made our own fun with the other children and each day was an adventure.

Word bank

Gumbaynggirr
siblings
Corindi
traditional
ceremonies
cultural
connections
community
Crown Land
employed
mattresses
chaff
hessian
electricity
tripod
endowment
cheque
luxuries
extended
oysters
worrying
adventure